CW00496825

Clairvoyance: Detailed Guide On Voluntary Clairvoyance

Psychic Development Of Seeing Using Voluntary Clairvoyance

By: Carin Weatherly

ISBN-13: 978-1481801454

Carin Weatherly

TABLE OF CONTENTS

Clairvoyance

Publishers Notes

Disclaimer

This publication is intended to provide helpful and informative material. It is not intended to diagnose, treat, cure, or prevent any health problem or condition, nor is intended to replace the advice of a physician. No action should be taken solely on the contents of this book. Always consult your physician or qualified health-care professional on any matters regarding your health and before adopting any suggestions in this book or drawing inferences from it.

The author and publisher specifically disclaim all responsibility for any liability, loss or risk, personal or otherwise, which is incurred as a consequence, directly or indirectly, from the use or application of any contents of this book.

Any and all product names referenced within this book are the trademarks of their respective owners. None of these owners have sponsored, authorized, endorsed, or approved this book.

Always read all information provided by the manufacturers' product labels before using their products. The author and publisher are not responsible for claims made by manufacturers.

Paperback Edition 2012

Manufactured in the United States of America

DEDICATION

I want to dedicate this book to my master teacher that helped me to control my psychic powers and clairvoyance and have done this book to help others.

CHAPTER 1- UNDERSTANDING THE BASICS OF CLAIRVOYANCE

Clairvoyance literally means *"clear sight"*. It is the skill to see or distinguish with the eye of mind things that are happening in a distant location without being aware of the event beforehand. A lot of the enthusiasts and professionals in the paranormal world are of the belief that the ability to be psychic is in all of us.

It is just waiting to be unlocked. They are of the belief that a lot of individuals do not choose to access this psychic ability due to the fact that they are not willing to develop it or may even be unaware that it exists.

There is a lot of dedication required to develop these clairvoyant abilities. On the other hand, each person is possessed with second sight but it has to be accessed.

There exist two forms of psychic abilities, involuntary and voluntary. The voluntary form of clairvoyance is typically seen as a positive aspect of the ability and the involuntary form of clairvoyance is typically seen as the negative, dark and dangerous aspect.

A lot of clairvoyants purport that the voluntary form is acquired through generous healthy living coupled with the readiness to access the inner part of your being to be able to see the invisible. The other form (involuntary) is something that one has no control over. It is believed that when the clairvoyance is involuntary the individual is typically thought to be open to danger and being taken over by a malevolent entity.

A lot of individuals that are in the process of honing their psychic abilities tend to believe that as soon as they make a bit of progress, they will be able to discern everything that is happening from that point onward.

The more proficient psychics advise that it is not as easy as that. They also advise that it requires a lot of dedicated cultivation of these abilities and taking heed of the necessary precautions to be able to connect voluntarily to the other dimension. It is also important to stay within the limits of one's ability and also be careful of the way in which the unseen energy is used as well.

Individuals that study clairvoyance state that it is an extremely dangerous thing to do and can let dark influences in. it is typically stated that in the world that we exist in (physical world) things do not change as they do in the other world (unseen world). The main point that they are trying to get across is that anyone that is interested in practicing clairvoyance has to not only take it seriously but also get the necessary training before they move on to the advanced stages.

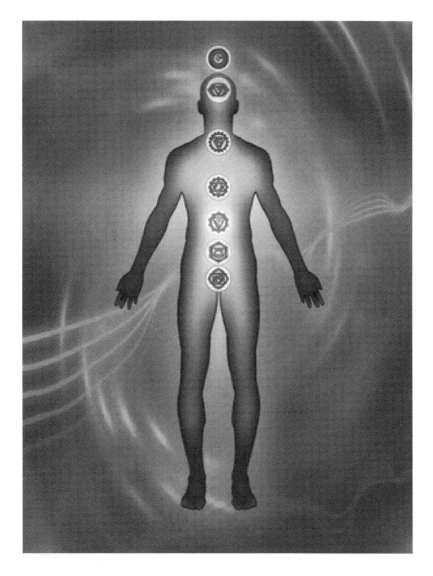

Some parapsychologists even suggest that we were all born with clairvoyant abilities and a lot of us stay in that state for at least the first twelve months of life. Contingent on the environment that one grew up in and the level of spiritual development that one has, an individual may keep the ability to be clairvoyant for a bit longer and then notice as it becomes less and less prevalent or just go away. These parapsychologists also state that it takes voluntary clairvoyance to be able to accurately and truly experience and be able to interpret this experience of the other world and also give advice to help prevent the accidental drift into involuntary clairvoyance.

More often than not the words psychic and clairvoyance are typically used to make reference to a number of clairvoyant experiences. They are outlined below:

Touching/Feeling (Clairsentience)

In the area of parapsychology, this is a kind of extra sensory perception in which an individual feels or touches things to get their psychic knowledge. To break the word down clair is a French word meaning "clear and sentience is of Latin origin (from sentire) and means *"to feel."*

Apart from that there is also a religious aspect to it all. For instance clairsentience in Buddhism represents one of the six special functions of humans. It is the skill that can be acquired when one gets to the expert level of meditation.

Typically the term is indicative of an individual that is able to sense the vibration of others. Varying degrees of this ability exist and can range from sensing an individual's thoughts or emotions or perceiving

Clairvoyance

diseases in others. This skill varies from the mind's eye in that there is formation of a visual in the mind.

Clairsentience is related to psychometry which literally means measuring the soul.

Listening/hearing (Clairaudience)

In parapsychology, this sensory perception which literally means clear hearing is a type of ability that enables an individual to gather information through auditory means. More often than not it is thought of as a type of clairvoyance. It is the skill to hear on a paranormal level as opposed to clairsentience (feeling) and clairvoyance (seeing).

Persons that have this gift are said to have hearing that is psi-mediated. It is not the actual hearing of noise but refers instead to what the inner mental ear picks up much in the same way that individuals perceive words without hearing anything. It may also denote the real awareness of sounds like noises, tones or voices that cannot be heard by any other individual or picked up by recording apparatus.

In Buddhism it is thought that those that are well versed in meditation and are now at a higher level of consciousness also have the ability to turn on that third ear and hear what is going on in the unseen world. this ability can clearly be differentiated from the voices that are heard by mentally ill persons as it tends to provide information that is not available normally (including magic tricks like cold readings) and as such is said to be a paranormal or psychic ability.

Smelling (Clairalience)

This ability is also known as clairescence. This is the ability to get clairvoyant input through the sense of smell.

Knowing (Claircognizance)

In parapsychology, knowing is a type of extra sensory perception that allows an individual to access information on the psychic level through knowledge. This refers to the skill to be aware of something without being able to explain why you do. It is similar to what mediums experience. The word claircognizance is from the French words "clair" and "conaissance" which means clear knowledge.

Tasting (Clairgustance)

In the area of parapsychology, this skill is said to be one in which an individual is able to taste something without actually placing something in their oral cavity. It is said that those that have this skill are capable of sensing something from the other realm through this extra sensory perception of tasting.

CHAPTER 2- HOW TO DEVELOP VOLUNTARY CLAIRVOYANT POWERS

Though you may not be a born clairvoyant, you still have the ability to develop the skills of clairvoyance. The fits thing that I did when I started developing my psychic skills was to work on my clairvoyant skills. I literally bought a book on psychic development and started to do the exercises in it to open the mind's eye.

I can say that the first exercise I outlined below did open up my mind's eye which is the core of the skill of clairvoyance. The only thing is that I got a bit scared and allowed it to close after a few days. I had started to perceive my spiritual guides in my third eye and also saw some other things moving. In addition to that I began to see auras around other persons and experienced some rather vivid dreams. I became rather overwhelmed as it was not something that I was used to.

Exercises to Develop Voluntary Clairvoyance

The exercise that I used is outlined below:

See oneself with a number of balloons in your hand, seven to be exact. They are colored indigo, violet, blue, green, yellow, orange and red. You should then let one balloon go at a time starting with the red one and watch them go up into the sky and when one disappears from sight let another go and so on until they are all gone.

If you are not familiar with the process of visualizing then this exercise might be a bit challenging for you initially. You might find it difficult to concentrate or find it hard to see things in color. It is all dependent on the level that your imaginative skills are at.

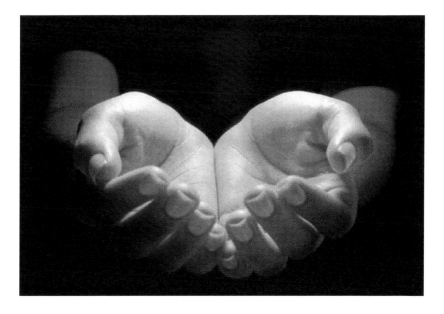

Any activity which makes use of one's visual imagination is great for improving upon ones clairvoyant abilities. This is due to the fact that your imagination serves as the means by which the spiritual beings convey information to you through the use of images.

The more receptive you are on that level, the easier it will be to receive these images. The question is how will you be able to determine what is from the spiritual being and what is merely your imagination running wild? When you get a visual message from a being you are not in control of that image. It pops up in the mind without you having anything to do with it.

Another method that you can use to develop your voluntary clairvoyant abilities is to imagine that the mind's eye is right between the eyebrows. After getting that image, work on opening it. Bear in mind that all the process of visualization does is to prepare you to do something specific. Regular practice of the form of visualization allows

Clairvoyance

you to focus your energy on opening the mind's eye which is the core
of the skill of clairvoyance.

Specific Exercises

Candles and Lamps

Take a few deep breaths then in a location that you find comfortable
sit on a chair and allow your muscles to relax. Then start to focus on a
light from a lamp or a candle that is not obstructed in any way. Start to
feel that energy going to your head, right to that area between the
eyebrows (where you visualized your mind's eye to be).

Remain focused until the thoughts recede by themselves and when
the mind is free from all that clutter, close your eyes. When the mind's
eye starts to become more active you will be able to see the light or
flame without your eyes being open. This can also be done with any
other object.

Fingers and Hands

Keeping the fingers about five centimeters apart place them in front of
your eyes. Slowly start to defocus. The vision will become blurred and
then start to clear after a while revealing a finger in between the two
fingers. That is the goal of this exercise. When you can visualize a
finger in between your actual fingers keep looking and work on seeing
a hand and wrist as well. This requires extremely high levels of
meditation and concentration.

Seeing Auras of Objects and Living Things

As best as you can relax your muscles while focusing on breathing
then move on to start concentrating on the area in between your

eyebrows and focus on what is in the background. This requires you to defocus and remain like this until you can visualize the lights.

Dragging the Light

Look at a flame or bulb and attempt to drag a line of that light or flame to you. If you are new to the practice it will take a bit of time to get the levels of concentration needed to be able to do this with ease.

Stages of clairvoyance

The first step of one's clairvoyant ability is gained in the world as we know it. The next level is acquired in what is known as the fourth dimension. The fourth dimension as well as the third can be found in the fifth dimension (astral and mental plane respectively) and the fifth dimension can be found the sixth (causal plane).

The ones that have no interest in having an understanding of what they go through daily will not be able to develop their abilities of clairvoyance. The ones that make the effort to have a bit more knowledge of the world that they live in have begun to awaken that ability and are able to begin exploring other planes.

Bear in mind that there are individuals that have acquired some level of knowledge in past lives and are reborn (reincarnated) with more highly developed skills of extra sensory perception. A lot of these individuals are born with these abilities but soon start to lose it and end up in a state of confusion.

One instance that can be used as an example is the set of children that are diagnosed as being schizophrenic or are prescribed drugs for hyperactivity as they are able to see and recant experiences they have in other planes. Not to say that schizophrenia does not exist or that hyperactivity does not exist but many that receive these diagnoses do not really have these conditions.

In the astral plane (fourth dimension) the possibility exists to see the aura of objects and living things. The ability exists to see the elements of nature and the faint energy that all objects emanate.

The next dimension (the fifth) is the level that one experiences dreams while the body itself is at rest. When one starts to have vision in this dimension, the persons will be able to make use of the opportunity to explore the metal and astral planes. Both these planes work specifically in this dimension.

The causal plane (sixth dimension) is where one consciousness that is free from ego exists. Once one is able to free ones consciousness from the trappings of ego one can have direct access to this plane of existence.   What Inhibits Clairvoyance?

A few individuals that are born clairvoyant may never ever discover that they have this gift. Anytime this occurs, it typically means that there is some sort of energy or block of the mind's eye. The root cause may bet that there something unpleasant or unexpected was seen and triggered some level of trauma.

On a personal note there are two main reasons why I do not place a lot of focus on the developing of my own clairvoyant abilities more than I have already. The first is that I do not need to have it and the next is that I really do not want to have the clear sight as I saw something that I did not want to see when I first started using this ability. I was about eight at the time and late in the night I was in my bed playing when I suddenly saw someone standing in the corner of my room looking right at me.

After that I remember covering my head with the sheets and hoping that this being would just go away. I was truly scared and remember that my heart was beating really fast. I made the decision then and there that I did not need this as seeing spirits was not all that I thought it would be.

A lot of other persons have challenges like this as a result of some sort of scary experience. If you are one of those individuals and you are able to remember the reason that triggered this inability to use the third eye you can always make use of particular exercises to start the process of healing.

The lack of ability or the unwillingness to accept the truth can also inhibit your ability to use your clairvoyant ability. For instance, if you dwell in a state of falsehood or denial the ability will start to fade. If your aim is to be able to develop that ability you have to come to terms with the truth and dispel any fallacies that you may have been holding on to. When you don't work on that level you will not trust your own intuition and perception and this will inhibit your clairvoyance.

Additional Tips:

You can place a clear quartz crystal or lapis lazuli over your mind's eye or you can go to a crystal shop to locate the crystal that you need to open this third eye. You will be drawn to the crystal that can enable this.

The initial stages of clairvoyance require you to close your eyes and make use of the mind's eye as opposed to being able to pick things up right away with ones physical eyes. One simply has to get rid of whatever trauma or fear that you have and affirm that you are clairvoyant and that it is safe to see.

CHAPTER 3- DEVELOPING CLAIRVOYANCE USING SCRYING

The process of scrying can be used to develop ones voluntary clairvoyant abilities. Scrying is carried out by placing the focus on something where symbols of the future, present or past can be seen. I have a crystal ball that my mother used to use when she did readings and I keep it tucked safely away in a storage bin along with the Tarot cards that she used to use.

This process has long been valued highly and is thought to be one of the original skills of divination as it can be found way back in our history.

A History of Scrying

What I appreciate about scrying is the fact that it has been in existence since the birth of civilization. It has been discovered by archaeologists that the graves of women from Catal Huyuk, the Neolithic city thought to be the birthplace of civilization contained polished obsidian discs. These are thought to be the ceremonial mirrors that the priestesses used for scrying. It is said that the Romans preferred crystals while the ancient Egyptians preferred the reflective surface of a pool of ink.

In the writings of Dr. John Dee, consultant to Queen Elizabeth the first and occultists made reference to enochian magic and the Golden Dawn which is an order of magic founded in the latter part of the nineteenth century. Both have references of scrying in their history but also have warning of doing it without the right level of preparation or overdoing it.

Increasing the Skills

Years of training are not required to develop the skills of scrying. It is however important to only do this practice when you are well versed in it and also to refrain from becoming too dependent on it.

Similar to other psychic abilities, the success that you can have with scrying is dependent on the ability to free your mind of all thought prompting any individual that I serious about this level of development of their psychic skills to practice meditation regularly.

When one is versed at freeing the mind, you can then select what you want to use for scrying. It could be a piece of crystal, a crystal ball or a mirror. Any object that is reflective can be used for scrying. You can also focus on a flame.

Once the object has been selected it should only be used for scrying and nothing else. If you are using flames, have a location in the home that you can safely light a fire for the purpose of scrying. The idea is to be able to have a line between ones everyday life and scrying sessions.

It is important to have a particular intention about what you hope to see. In the initial stages you can ask a friend or family member to put something in their home that you can try to find through this process. You may even want to try to determine what is going to happen at a particular time in the future. It can safely be done and one should always remember not to violate someone else's privacy.

A quiet location should be found where you will not be disturbed then you should get comfortable breathe and relax after setting up whatever you will be using for scrying. When settled focus on the object slightly defocusing your physical eyes and waiting for the process to unfold.

Do not be deterred if nothing happens for a period of time. Keep on practicing and after a while you will start to see symbols, images and scenes playing out. It may seem as if you are daydreaming. Allow your mind to remain calm while going through this experience or you can lose the vision if you try to do anything. When the mind starts to wander you should end the session.

You can clap your hands or stamp your feet to become grounded and end the session. Keep a journal where you can write down what you saw particularly those that require you to do some additional research. If you had enlisted a friend or family members help check with them to see if you saw correctly.

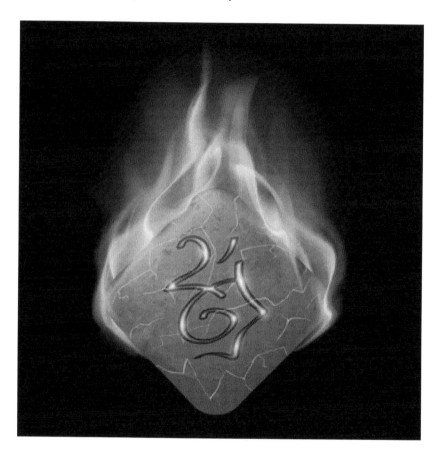

Another thing to bear in mind with this practice is that is opens a portal to "all that is." Anything that you see might be connected to something on the past, the present or the future. To make it even more complicated, it may also be possible to become a victim of your own visions so that is why it is prudent to keep a journal so that you are able to do a personal progress report.

What Can Scrying Be Used for?

Apart from using it to better develop your clairvoyant abilities one of the most obvious uses of the practice is to find things that are lost even though you have to be at a certain level to be able to do this. Remember though that this is something that on should not become dependent on. The best time to use this is when you really need the help to figure something out.

Einstein himself referred to the importance of creating a mental space to facilitate insight. Paul Dirac, a physicist and Nobel Prize winner is said to have received inspiration while trying to decipher an intricate theory while he was gazing into a fire. As such if you have a particular difficult project working on you can make use of scrying.

CHAPTER 4- HOW TO SEE CLEARY AND READ ENERGY

When I was a child, I was of the impression that clairvoyants were able to see the future with some special gift. I also thought that they must have some invisible eye that was unique to them. When I started to do a few courses on spiritual awareness I discovered that we all possessed this ability to see using this third eye (sixth chakra).

More important than that I found out the true meaning of clairvoyance which I have outlined in the first chapter. To recap it is not being physically able to read the future but to see life from a spiritual plane as opposed to using conditioning, beliefs, emotions and intellect.

One does become empowered when gifted with the ability to see beyond the reactivity and the physical right through to the realness of particular situations. The level of self awareness is enhanced allowing you to be able to start fresh after letting go of the past and healing old wounds. You have the ability to view the true dynamics of energy in groups and relationships as well as behind patterns that are not healthy.

To become voluntarily clairvoyant and open that third eye, have the ability to read energy and see clearly you can try what is outlined below:

Center within Your Mind's Eye

A lot of individuals often look at situations and people using a form of analysis linked to their heart chakra or another part of their energy system or body. This will cause some distortion of reality. This analyzer or intellect is great to get research done, compile data and categorize it. It is of much use beyond this. This chakra can be used to make

Clairvoyance

connections with persons but if there is any wound from love or heartache, what you perceive will be distorted.

The one place that you can have a clear perception of reality if through the use of your third eye and your spiritual being. From here you have the ability to see the whole aspect of a situation or a person. This sense of awareness exists in the center of the head, just a few inches away from the forehead. This is the location that most persons focus in on during the process of meditation. Take a note of the calmness and stillness that exists. Take a look at your life and your own self from this level to gain more clarity can become more self aware.

See the Energy in You

As stated throughout the gift of clairvoyance is a wonderful tool to make use of to improve upon spiritual growth and awareness. You can try to focus in on your mind's eye after closing your eyes (see chapter two). Start to see yourself as a spiritual entity being held in a human body, then greet this version of yourself. After that start to visualize a rose in front of you and fill the petals of the rose as it blossoms with your current life experiences, growth or lessons.

Visualize the color and shape of the rose and then take a look at the energy- don't start to think about it just observe the message, mood or tone. It may be a simple word or a feeling that comes to you. Release the image of the rose and open your eyes.

Interpret the Energy of a Situation

Energy can be found in every business, home, relationship, situation and individual. As you become more adept at reading energy you will have clearer sight. You can once again use the image of the rose or anything else to see the energy in various things. For instance if you want to examine the relationship between you and someone else visualize it in the rose. Make use of your mind's eye and not your analytical eye and make a note of the essence of the rose and also note what images or feelings come to mind that represent that relationship.

Clairvoyance

This will give you a good start on learning how to use your powers of clairvoyance to do an energy reading and to see clearly. One simply has to be patient and trust in you. There is something to bear in mind when reading the future and reading others. When you read the future, only look at the next step as a means to confirm your spiritual and personal growth.

If you make the attempt to read more into the future, you might start to believe that you have no other options. Things are constantly changing (particularly for those on a journey to conscious spiritual awareness. So there exist a lot of possibilities and probabilities available. Have enough trust in yourself to select what is best for you at the particular time.

When reading the energy of others or trying to determine the energy dynamics they possess, it is imperative that you have healthy boundaries of energy, be in control of your space and be aware of the way in which to release the energy that others have from your space.

Once you have discovered that you have this particular gift and decide to develop it always remember that it is to be taken in steps. One should also bear the various warnings that you will be made aware of during the learning process.

CHAPTER 5- DANGERS OF CLAIRVOYANCE

Having the power of clairvoyance is an extremely great benefit that has its own unique set of advantages. If this gift is used correctly it can really help the individual that posses it. On the other hand if it is not used correctly it can be more of a curse and a hindrance. The main dangers associated with the misuse of the powers of clairvoyance arise from impurity, ignorance and pride. If these are kept at bay, you will benefit greatly from the gift.

The primary form of danger is associated with pride. Every human being has some level of pride and it does manifest on occasion. For the clairvoyant however feelings of pride can lead him to think that he is superior to his fellowman.

He may see himself as being specially selected for some task assigned by a higher power, blessed with a gift that will never make them make errors and so on.

It has to be remembered that there are a number of malevolent and sportive entities on the spiritual plane that are waiting to fill the mind with these delusions of grandeur, to embody and reflect the thoughts of same and to play the role of whichever spirit guide or archangel that is called upon.

Suffice it to say that it is extremely easy to convince someone that he is really the best there is and more than worthy of this spiritual contact even though his family and friends may have been aloof to these gifs and as such failed to appreciate that aspect of the individual.

Ignorance then comes to the fore as the other dangerous aspect to the practice of clairvoyance. If the individual is familiar with the subject from a historical point of view or has a comprehension of the rules governing the spiritual planes from which he gets his visions he will not be able to say that he is the only one that is blessed with this particular gift.

He also cannot be smug about not making mistakes. When this occurs, as it does quite often the possibility exists to make any number of mistakes on what he actually perceives and also to be subject to all kinds of malicious entities from the fifth dimension (astral plane).

This individual has no set criteria to judge what is seen or even thinks that he sees and no test that can be applied to these communications and visions and as such he has no means of the proportion of things and then tends to put truth into a small bit of divine wisdom. In addition to that in a bid to understand subjects based on science, he may tend to totally misinterpret what he is actually seeing and as a consequence will seriously broadcast things that are ludicrous.

The next danger is impurity. The individual that has pure intentions and has pure thoughts and lives a pure life free from selfishness has a natural guard against the malicious entities that dwell on the spiritual planes. This individual would possess nothing that they could use as a form of manipulation and as such would serve no purpose to them. Conversely all the naturally good influences that surround this individual would use him as a conduit through which they can communicate and as such a next barrier would be forms protecting him from all that is evil and low. The individual that is not pure will, on the other hand be open to an d literally attract all the bad that is in the spiritual plane and will respond to it quite easily while not being easily influenced by the good forces that exist.

The voluntary clairvoyant that takes all of these things into consideration and makes a concerted effort to stay away from it will also make the effort to learn about the history and the true purpose of clairvoyance. This individual will remain humble and keep his motives pure and will be able to learn from the very powers that he has been blessed with and as such be able to use them rather effectively.

Having initially taken paid attention to developing his character to be better able to make a note of any visions that he may have he will be able to take the time necessary to decipher the truth from all the information that he is receiving by doing the necessary checks and balances required to determine same.

Clairvoyance

Through this process he will soon be able to quickly get some sort of order out of all the chaos and also learn how to know what to trust in and what to disregard as information that is simply unintelligible.

Over a period of time this clairvoyant will discover that he will receive impressions, either through clear sight or by feeling about the individuals that he has contact with. Journaling this information as it comes and doing the necessary checks and balances when possible will soon reveal how much reliability can be placed in these impressions and as soon as this is determined he will make great progress as he will now be in possession of a gift that allows him to be of much more use to those he is providing assistance to than he could have been if he had simply viewed them with the physical eyes.

If, for instance, this gift of sight comes with the ability to see auras, he will be able to make judgments on how best to deal with these individuals and how to uncover and build upon their good qualities, to suppress what is not desirable in their characters and to make then stronger.

Once more, this ability might often allow him to see something of the inner workings of nature, to perceive something of the process of evolutions that surround us and are non human. This will enable the acquisition of the most precious knowledge on a myriad of subjects. Should it happen that he is linked to another clairvoyant that has higher abilities through regular training it will be an even greater advantage as he will be able to get help with the visions interpreted by one he can rely on.

In general, the path that is recommended to the new clairvoyant is one that entails great skills of observation and lots of patience. This individual should also make the best use of this gift that they have been blessed with and keep all the negative aspects of this practice suppressed. After a while he will get the necessary training required and be able to become one of the people that can provide help with proper guidance from a spiritual dimension.

Specialized training ought to be arranged in the early stages for children that are clairvoyant. The current educational system has a tendency to repress psychic abilities and a lot of young individuals tend to be taken up with their schoolwork. In the past, in Rome and Greece and child that as deemed to be clairvoyant were immediately isolated as postulants or vestal virgins and received specialized training. Nowadays it is typical to ignore these abilities and not just from an educational perspective.

The most apt way to prevent the loss of this gift is to place the gifted in a type of monastery where they can learn what they need to know and live what they learn as well as being in regular setting will not encourage this development. If traits of clairvoyance are determined they ought to be developed.

Individuals that are psychic from birth typically make use of something known as etheric sight. This is the ability to perceive physical matter in a different form while not yet able to see the matter present on the astral plane. When they observe a physical thing however such as an exposed section of the human body like the hand or the fact they tend to see a number of tiny forms like double pyramids, stars or dice.

These are not a part of the astral plane or a plane of thought but instead belong to the etheric section of the physical form. It is simply the very tiny discharges from the body, waste composed of salts hat are finely divided and are constantly being released by the body. What is perceived may be different for a number of reasons. Primarily the loss of health can change them but changes in emotions can also have an effect on them. Even certain trains of thought can cause changes.

Lastly note that it should not always be assumed that an individual that perceives something associated with a higher plane is clairvoyant. Through clairvoyance for instance you may perceive an apparition but bear in mind that there are a number of other ways that an individual can see or assume that he sees something that is an apparition.

ABOUT THE AUTHOR

With the book **Carin Weatherly** demonstrates that she really did her research by zoning in on the positive side of clairvoyance which is voluntary. She gives not only a sound working definition of the topic but goes a step further to include all the information that one could ever need to learn as much as you can about the topic without flooding the mind with too much information to assimilate.

Carin always had an interest in the paranormal and she focused her interests on clairvoyance when she realized that there was more to it than she first thought. She then made the decision to find out as much as she could and then after she collated all the information to share it through writing.

She is aware that there are many naysayers and can only encourage all to read and form their own opinion after they get to know more about the practice. After all one cannot discredit what one knows nothing about. She does get a lot of persons to satiate their curiosity by reading her book.

She does not push a particular concept on the reader but leaves them to make their own informed decision at the end of it all.

13758999R00019

Printed in Great Britain
by Amazon